The ULTIMATE,
grab-a-PEN,
get-the-WORDS-right,
have-a-BLAST
WRITING BOOK

Write Now!

JOE RHATIGAN
with Rain Newcomb &
Veronika Alice Gunter

LARK BOOKS
A Division of Sterling Publishing Co., Inc.
New York

Art Direction,
Design, & Production:
Celia Naranjo

Proofreader:
Karen Levy

Library of Congress Cataloging-in-Publication Data

Rhatigan, Joe.
  Write now! : the ultimate, grab-a-pen, get-the-words-right, have-a-blast
writing book / by Joe Rhatigan with Rain Newcomb and Veronika Alice Gunter ;
illustrated by Barbara Pollak.— 1st ed.
      p. cm.
  Includes index.
  ISBN 1-57990-621-4 (pbk.)
  1. Authorship. I. Newcomb, Rain. II. Gunter, Veronika Alice. III. Title.
PN147.R567 2005
808'.02—dc22

                                    2004022442

10 9 8 7 6 5 4 3 2 1

First Edition

Published by Lark Books, A Division of
Sterling Publishing Co., Inc.
387 Park Avenue South, New York, N.Y. 10016

© 2005, Lark Books
Illustrations © 2005, Barbara Pollak

Distributed in Canada by Sterling Publishing,
c/o Canadian Manda Group, 165 Dufferin Street
Toronto, Ontario, Canada M6K 3H6

Distributed in the U.K. by Guild of Master Craftsman Publications Ltd.,
Castle Place, 166 High Street, Lewes, East Sussex, England BN7 1XU
Tel: (+ 44) 1273 477374, Fax: (+ 44) 1273 478606,
e-mail: pubs@thegmcgroup.com,
Web: www.gmcpublications.com

Distributed in Australia by Capricorn Link (Australia) Pty Ltd.,
P.O. Box 704, Windsor, NSW 2756 Australia

If you have questions or comments about this book, please contact:
Lark Books
67 Broadway
Asheville, NC 28801
(828) 253-0467

Manufactured in China

ISBN 1-57990-621-4

For information about custom editions, special sales, premium and corporate
purchases, please contact Sterling Special Sales Department at 800-805-5489
or specialsales@sterlingpub.com.

Contents

The Most Interesting Introduction Ever!

We, the authors, have about 10 seconds to grab you by the shirt and scream,

"Keep reading this introduction. It's interesting!"

Still reading? We certainly hope so—especially because we spent a lot of time writing, thinking, rewriting, rereading, and polishing that first paragraph. We made sure we had an attention-getting title. And how about the first sentence? Did it make you want to read more?

Ten seconds is about how long it takes people to decide whether or not they're going to keep reading something. And boy do we have our work cut out for us. Why? Well, the introduction is the part of the book where the author writes a bunch of stuff about how and why his or her book is soooo cool. But, we're pretty sure almost nobody ever reads introductions, because most of them are about as interesting as Aunt Ida and Uncle Bob's slide show of their two-week cruise to Bora Bora (otherwise known as Borin' Borin').

Writing is a lot about making decisions. Did the Aunt Ida and Uncle Bob slide show reference work? We thought it did, and that's why we left it in. As a writer, you're faced with decisions like that all the time. You have to choose the words you think best describe what you're trying to say. You decide the order of those words to make your writing clear and interesting. You figure out what's coming next, what's okay to leave out, and what must stay in. That's what writing's all about. We wrote this book to help you with all your writing decisions, from finding something good to write about to making sure your main character has something interesting to do in your story.

What's in This Book

●✦ Lots of space to do your own brainstorming, thinking, writing, and revising

●✦ Tons of ideas for finding cool topics to write about

●✦ Valuable tools to get you writing again when you get stuck

●✦ Revising and editing techniques to make your writing better

●✦ Thoughts, ideas, opinions, writing tricks, and snide remarks from three professional writers who spend most of their time thinking about their writing decisions

Time for a Quiz!
(We hate quizzes, but this one's easy.)

Place a check mark next to each statement that applies to you:

☐ I want to write about stuff I care about.

☐ I want to play with words, sentences, and paragraphs until they say exactly what I want them to say.

☐ I want to have fun while figuring out how to be a better writer.

If you checked none out of three: You should still read this book, if only to realize that you can write about things you care about and not just boring stuff like that famous "What I Did During Summer Vacation" essay you wrote on an envelope five minutes before it was due. You've come to the right place.

If you checked one out of three: We bet you picked #3. Everyone wants to have fun, and there's no reason you can't turn writing into something you enjoy doing. Even people who hate writing grocery lists can learn to enjoy writing. You've come to the right place.

If you checked two out of three: You probably bought this book with your allowance. That's cool. Which of the three choices don't you want to do? Read them again. I bet you really want to do that third one, but you're just being difficult. You've come to the right place.

If you checked three out of three: You either checked two and we made you change your answer (see the paragraph above) or you already like writing and want to get better at it. You, also, have come to the right place.

How to Use This Book

Bet you're itching to write something in this book.
Go ahead. That's what all the blank lines are for.

Is this where you usually get stuck when you're writing? You're not alone; most writers feel that from time to time. We call this UIWTWBISAAB-PACTOASTTWA (which is short for "Ugh-I-want-to-write-but-I'm-staring-at-a-blank-page-and-can't-think-of-a-single-thing-to-write-about") Syndrome. So if you suffer from UIWTWI ... whatever Syndrome, **Chapter 1: Ready, Set, Write!** on pages 10 to 49 will cure you, and you'll find plenty of topics you care about at your fingertips.

Some writers get stuck around here. You start off well, writing and writing and writing—and then BAM. You're stuck with a major case of "I-don't-know-where-to-go-next." Some writers call this Writer's Block. Don't worry; it's not infectious. A healthy dose of **Chapter 2: Are You Stuck?** on pages 50 to 83 will get you through this hump and all the way to the end of your story, poem, essay, or whatever you're writing.

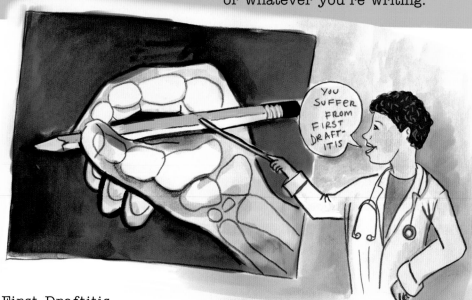

Of course, you're not done just because you've filled up all the blank lines and reached the end. If you think you're done, then you're suffering from First Draftitis, which is what you get when you think your first draft is perfect and ready for publication. A shot or two of **Chapter 3: Getting Better All the Time** on pages 84 to 119 will get you thinking about your first draft as just the beginning of your writing journey.

Now, turn the page, and start reading and writing. You can work through this book page by page, or you can skip around when you know you need help with something specific. You can use the activities to work on a piece of writing you've already started, to find an idea, or to polish your final draft. By the way, if you come across a writing term you don't understand, check out **Words That Matter** on page 127. Have fun!

Chapter 1

Ready, Set, Write!

YOU'VE SHARPENED YOUR PENCILS UNTIL ALL THAT'S LEFT ARE THE ERASERS.

You've dusted off your computer, checked your e-mail 53 times, and made sure each button on your keyboard works. You're ready to write.

But you have nothing to write about.

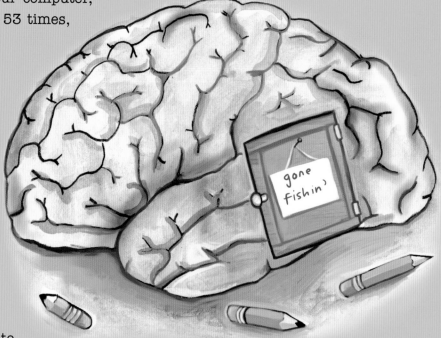

That's usually enough of a reason to keep 90 percent of would-be writers from ever writing a word. You're different, though. You REALLY want to write. Well, here are a couple of writing secrets you should know about:

My brain doesn't work!

- Writers aren't born knowing what to write about.

- Writers don't wake up every morning, sit at their desks, and instantly start writing or typing their next best-selling novel, short story, essay, or news article.

- Sure there are days when inspiration hits, the pen starts moving, and bingo, a great idea is sitting right there. But then there are times when even the most famous writers in the world have nothing. You knock on your brain and nobody's home.

Good writers know they won't always have something up their sleeve. So what do they do? They create lists. They walk around with notepads in their pockets so when a good idea hits, they can write it down before they forget it. They keep writing notebooks. They play word games. They read books, magazines, newspapers, shampoo bottles... just about anything. They think about stuff they care about. They learn how to pay attention to the world. This chapter will help you do all these things—and more.

Take the First Step.

Read through this chapter. Do the activities right here in this book. By the time you get to the end of the chapter, you'll have scores of lists, thoughts, and, best of all, ideas. You'll have created your very own idea bank. So, stop sharpening those poor pencils and get started!

Ugh!
I have nothing
to write about!

I had this great idea in the shower this morning, but now I can't remember what it was.

How does J. K. Rowling do it?

Write What You Know

Right now, you're probably thinking, "Yeah, yeah, yeah. Everybody says, 'Write what you know,' but nothing I know is worth writing about." That's not true. The reason so many writing teachers say to "write what you know" is because if it's interesting to you, there's a good chance you can make it interesting to your readers.

If you know a lot about a particular time in history, such as the Middle Ages, you can create a fictional character who witnesses all the excitement of the times. Or if you know a lot about a particular subject—say, magic— you could write a bunch of things about that.

Example Time:

Something I Know About: Magic

How I can include what I know in my writing:

I could…

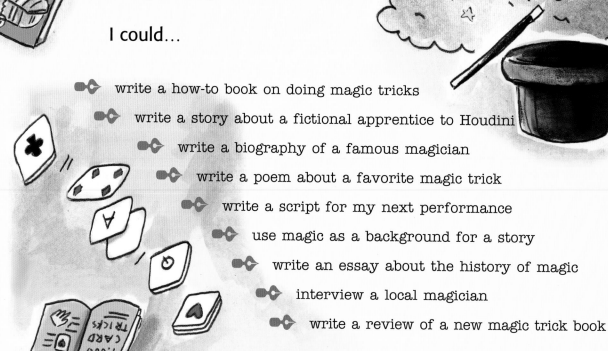

- write a how-to book on doing magic tricks
- write a story about a fictional apprentice to Houdini
- write a biography of a famous magician
- write a poem about a favorite magic trick
- write a script for my next performance
- use magic as a background for a story
- write an essay about the history of magic
- interview a local magician
- write a review of a new magic trick book

Now you try it. Make a list of topics and things you know about. Don't think too much about it. Just write things down as they come to you. Keep adding to it whenever you think of something else. (It could be minutes, hours, days, or even weeks later.)

✎ _____   _____   _____

_____   _____   _____

_____   _____   _____

_____   _____   _____

_____   _____   _____

_____   _____   _____

Next, choose one of the topics you came up with and make a list of all the different things you might be able to write on that topic.

✎ _____

_____

_____

_____

_____

_____

_____

_____

_____

LIST MANIA!

Everyone loves lists. Lists get us through the grocery store without forgetting essential ingredients for our famous homemade pizza recipe. They remind us of what we have to do for homework. Best of all, creating lists helps writers think of things to write about. Start some lists of your own, and don't give up after one or two items. Keep thinking and writing. Your brain might surprise you.

Groceries
Onions
peppers
Green Olives
Black Olives
Mushrooms
Anchovies
pineapple
Feta cheese
Capers
pepperoni
Chicken
Sausage
Spam
Jalapeños
Ham

 List o' Things You Like or Care About

It could be a sport you play, a person, a pet, melting polar caps...you name it!

_____   _____

_____   _____

_____   _____

 Stuff I Wish I Knew More About

This might be something you heard on the news and didn't quite understand or something your teacher said in science class that interested you.

_____   _____

_____   _____

_____   _____

✎ **Things That Make Me Nervous**

_____   _____

_____   _____

_____   _____

_____   _____

✎ **Times I've Gotten in Big Trouble**

_____   _____

_____   _____

_____   _____

_____   _____

✎ **Stupid Things I've Done**

_____   _____

_____   _____

_____   _____

_____   _____

✎ **Things My Friends Do That Make Me Mad**

_____   _____

_____   _____

_____   _____

_____   _____

✎ **Pros and Cons of Being the Youngest, Oldest, Middle, or Only Child**

_____   _____

_____   _____

_____   _____

_____   _____

Did you find anything promising here? Even if you think not, leave these lists alone and come back to them someday. Something that looks boring now may spark an idea later on. Good writers never throw anything away (much to their families' horror).

Freewriting

**No, this doesn't mean that other types of writing cost money.
Here's how to overcome Blank Page Syndrome!**

Place your pen on the first blank line on this page. Write something. Write anything. And don't stop writing until you fill up these pages. Don't even lift the pen from the paper! If you can't do it for yourself, do it for the thousands of writers out there who have nothing to write about. Ready? Go!

✎ _____

_____

_____

_____

What? You have nothing to write about? That's okay. Write, "I have nothing to write about!" as many times as you have to. Or pretend you're a dog and write, "Bark, bark, bark..." Whatever. Go ahead.

✎ _____

_____

_____

_____

_____

_____

_____

(Keep going!)

Remember this: Freewriting is not supposed to be good writing.

_____

_____

_____

_____

_____

_____

_____

_____

_____

_____

_____

_____

_____

Finished? Felt good, didn't it?

Did you have to write "I have nothing to write about" the whole time? Or did something else come to you? Were you happy when you got to the bottom of the page, or did you feel like you could write more? Go back and read what you wrote. Are there some ideas you could turn into something more?

This is called **freewriting**, and writers use it sometimes when they need a way to unlock their brains. Sometimes a phrase in your freewriting might turn into a topic for a great essay or piece of dialogue. Turn the page for more on freewriting.

WADING THROUGH THE MUCK

The best thing about freewriting is that you can write anything that comes into your head without worrying. After some practice, you may find that ideas come pouring out of your pen. Even your first attempt may have given you ideas. Reread your freewriting on pages 16 and 17, and write down any ideas that came up. If you wrote, "bark, bark" the whole time, perhaps you can write down, "Sometimes I feel like a dog."

Next time, try writing for five minutes straight. Set a timer if you need to. Once you get good at it, try it for 10 minutes. Then 15. After a while, see how long you can write without stopping.

Dialogue for Complete Strangers

Find a magazine with lots of interesting pictures in it. Cut out various people and place them randomly under the dialogue balloons. Tape them in place. Invent dialogue for these "characters." See whether at least one of these unlikely pairs strikes up a conversation that leads to a story.

Ripped from the Headlines!

When the writers of a TV crime drama can't come up with a good story, where do they turn? To newspapers, of course. And when they find a good story, they change the names to protect the innocent (and guilty), alter it to make it even more exciting, and then say the show is RIPPED FROM THE HEADLINES! Your story or main character can be RIPPED FROM THE HEADLINES! too.

Touchdown!

Avalanche!

Step 1: Find a newspaper, and rip out some stories that you like. Write down the details of the story that fascinated you.

_____

_____

_____

_____

_____

Step 2: Write down characteristics of one or two people that interested you.

_____

_____

_____

_____

_____

Lies!!!

Voting Fraud?

Step 3: Change the plot so you like the story even better.

Step 4: Start your first draft here.

Murder!!

Once Upon a Time

Old stories and fairy tales are excellent places to find inspiration for your own writing. These stories remain popular because they say something true about how bad and how good life can be. We can all relate to that. Grab a fairy tale or folk tale and make it your own!

Modernize it. If Sleeping Beauty were alive today, what would cause her to fall asleep? Because "prince" isn't really a profession anymore, what would the prince do for a living?

Change the setting. What if Little Red Riding Hood took place in New York City?

Pick up the story after, "And they lived happily ever after." Did Cinderella really enjoy a life of luxury with her prince?

Write the story from a different character's point of view. If the wicked stepsisters wrote the story, what would Cinderella be like? How would a munchkin tell the story of the Wizard of Oz?

Try a different point of view entirely—one that's not even human!

How would the beanstalk feel about Jack's adventures?

Jot down ideas of your own or take one of the ideas on the previous page and run with it.

_____
_____
_____
_____
_____
_____
_____
_____
_____
_____
_____
_____
_____
_____
_____
_____
_____
_____

Here are some great books that are rewritten famous tales:

Beauty: A Retelling of the Story of Beauty and the Beast, Robin McKinley; *Ella Enchanted*, Gail Carson Levine; *The Fairy's Mistake*, Gail Carson Levine; *The Magic Circle*, Donna Jo Napoli; *Sleeping Ugly*, Jane Yolen; *The Stinky Cheese Man and Other Fairly Stupid Tales*, Jon Scieszka; and *The Trial of Goldilocks*, Joseph Robinette.

You're one of the easiest things to write about. After all, who knows you better than you? Lots of people have written autobiographies. Think your life is too boring to be written about? Wrong! You've done plenty of story-worthy things in your life. Here are some ideas to get you started.

What's up with your family? Nobody's family is perfect, and writers can usually spend their whole careers just writing about their zany families.

What changes have happened in your life, and how did they affect your family?

✎ _____

_____

_____

Jot down a personal success story and how it made your feel.

✎ _____

_____

_____

_____

Write about a time you failed at something.

✎ _____

_____

_____

_____

Can you pinpoint the moment in your life when you realized you were no longer a child? Coming-of-age novels describe the events that cause their protagonist (your main character) to grow up. What would the coming-of-age novel of your life be like?

✎ _____

_____

_____

_____

_____

Turn your story into fiction. This is easy. Start writing your life story, then every time it gets boring, lie. Just don't try to pass this off as what really happened. And don't forget to change names to protect the innocent.

Ready, Set, Write!

Random List Story Starters

Stuck for an idea? Pick out random words and create a story that uses them. Take one item from each of the columns below and create a story with the four items you chose. And don't blame us if you end up with a story about your grandma playing chess on a pirate ship.

dusty suitcase	pet rock	Gila monster	flashlight
coffee mug	old gym socks	math teacher	swimming pool
ice cream	Australia	pirate ship	superhero
duct tape	6,542	spoon	earthworm
crackers	ducks	rocket ships	fireworks
diamonds	eggshells	mummies	grass
post office	candy store	gymnasium	park
werewolf	nerdy genius	mermaid	map
ants	skateboard	limousine	velociraptor
dragon	scooter	golf ball	tomato
cheese	chess board	library	roller coaster
grandma	mailman	inner tube	tricycle
deserted island	oil	bus driver	bully

✎ Write notes for your story here.

Get Unstuck with Magnets

Start a favorite word collection.

Once you have a bunch of cool words, type them on the computer in rows, and then print them on magnetic paper. (You can get printable magnetic sheets at craft stores and office supply centers.) Cut the words out, put them in a tin, and take them out when you're looking for inspiration. These are great for getting a poem off the ground or for finding the perfect description.

Here are some cool words we've come across over time. Look them up if you like them.

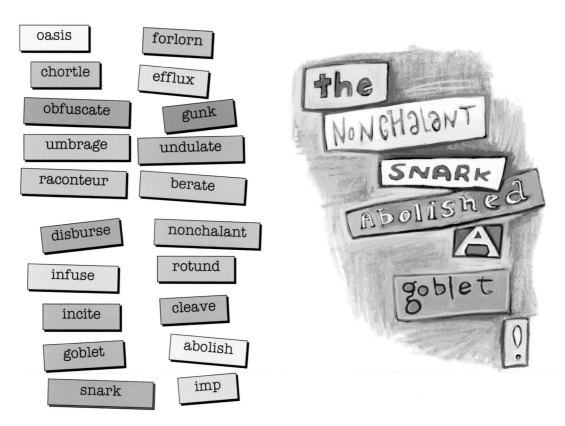

Include lots of articles ("the," "and," etc.), pronouns ("I," "you," "she," etc.), and prepositions ("to," "from," "in," etc.).

Also cut out some blanks for words you need to finish sentences.

For even more help, type a favorite song, poem, or nursery rhyme. Print it on the magnetic paper, cut out the words, and see what poems or cool sentences you can come up with using only the words of the piece you just printed.

Ready, Set, Write!

Keep a list of awesome words here. When you have a bunch, start your magnet collection.

The Tragic flaw

Achilles had that weak heel; Superman loses his powers around Kryptonite. Hey, everybody's got a tragic flaw, especially heroes. And it's a good thing, too, because tragic flaws are such handy plot devices.

A tragic flaw is the one bad thing in your otherwise perfect—or nearly perfect—hero. It's the undoing not only of your hero, but also of the whole plot. What happens when your hydrophobic (afraid of water) hero has to cross a river to save the world? Drama, conflict, and excitement, that's what!

Here's a list of some tragic flaws:

Fear of bathing	Greed	Uncontrollable anger
Fear of cars	Inability to lie (compulsion to tell the truth)	Uncontrollable obsession with cheese
Fear of cats		
Fear of snakes	Jealousy	Vanity (interest in appearance)
Fear of water	Laziness	
Fear of writing	Pride	

Come up with some flaws.

_____ _____ _____

_____ _____ _____

_____ _____ _____

_____ _____ _____

Create a hero, and then give him or her one tragic flaw.

✎ _____

_____

_____

_____

_____

_____

_____

Now, think of ways your character's tragic flaw can lead him or her into some bad situations.

✎ _____

_____

_____

_____

_____

_____

Plot ideas that come to mind.

✎ _____

_____

_____

_____

_____

_____

_____

_____

Change History

Rewriting history is great for the imagination.
"What if!" questions can give you a start for essays or stories.

What would the world be like if dinosaurs still roamed the earth?

What if Columbus didn't discover the Americas? What if people from the Americas discovered Europe first?

_____

_____

_____

_____

_____

_____

_____

What if the Internet hadn't been invented? How about cell phones?

_____

_____

_____

_____

_____

_____

What if television, or video games, had never been invented?

_____

_____

_____

_____

_____

_____

What if the Hubble Space Telescope discovered life on another planet?

_____

_____

_____

_____

_____

_____

_____

What if you left for school three minutes late? How might your day be different?

_____

_____

_____

_____

_____

_____

_____

What if your parents had never met each other?

_____

_____

_____

_____

_____

_____

What Writers Write

There are tons of ways to write about your ideas. Here are a few.

Advertisement

Advice column

Article

Autobiography

Biography

Book review

CD review

Comic book

Comic strip

Descriptive essay

Diary entry

E-mail to friends

Essay

Fairy tale

Fantasy

Fiction

Graphic novel

Greeting card

History book

Horror novel

Illustrated children's book

Instructions

Interview

Letter to the editor

Literary criticism

Magazine article

Memoir

Movie review

Mystery novel

Myth

Newspaper column

Novel

Novella (short novel)

Opinion column

Oral history recording

Parody

Personal essay

Persuasive essay

Play

Play review

Poem

Profile

Puppet show

Radio play

Report on current events

Research article

Satirical essay

Science fiction novel

Screenplay

Script

Short story

Skit

Song

Speech

Sports announcer's script

Stand-up comedy routine

Textbook

Thriller

TV script

TV show review

Website

From Photographs to Paragraphs

Have you ever heard the expression "A picture is worth a thousand words"? Well, how about writing a thousand words about a picture? Pictures can be a wonderful way to get a story started.

Ask your parents or grandparents whether they have any old family photos kicking around. Look through the photos you gather until you find one that sparks your interest. Start by answering the questions below, but don't feel like you have to keep to the truth. Let your imagination take over—that's the trick here. After answering the questions, see whether you can freewrite about the photograph.

What do you think is going on? _____

_____

_____

Who's taking the picture? _____

_____

_____

_____

What's the occasion? _____

_____

_____

✏️ How are the people in the picture relating to each other? _____

_____

_____

_____

_____

✏️ What happened before the picture was taken? _____

_____

_____

_____

_____

_____

✏️ What happened after the picture was taken? _____

_____

_____

_____

✏️ Is there anything mysterious about the picture? _____

_____

_____

_____

_____

Try this same activity with a work of art. Go to a museum (they often have free admission days!) or get an art book out of the library. Not sure which artist to check out first? Try Edward Hopper. His paintings tell stories almost by themselves.

Listen In

Spend the day listening in on other people's conversations. Write down bits of conversations you overhear. You can do this in front of the TV if you really have to. Simply sit there, and don't watch, but listen.

she likes who?!?
You look like a ROCK STAR
in those shoes...
...*in BIG trouble*
...*Grounded for LIFE*...
CAUGHT cheating on the MATH test...

✎ Write a line or two of conversation.

_____

_____

_____

_____

_____

_____

✎ Start a response or a reply to it here. _____

_____

_____

_____

_____

_____

_____

_____

✎ Write some more overheard lines of conversation. _____

_____

_____

_____

_____

✎ Imagine a response here. _____

_____

_____

_____

_____

✎ Jot down some juicy gossip you overheard. _____

_____

_____

_____

✎ Then what? _____

_____

_____

_____

_____

From Rags to Riches

A classic story line is one in which your protagonist has to overcome certain obstacles to reach his or her dreams. This is often called a "Rags to Riches" story, and the obstacles the main character faces almost seem destined to defeat him or her.

Example Time

From New Kid at School to Famous Recording Artist

From Painfully Shy Loner to Superhero

From C Student to A student

From Airhead Cheerleader to President

Come up with some of your own.

From _____ to _____

From _____ to _____

From _____ to _____

Now pick one you like, and do a quick freewrite of a possible story by answering these questions.

Who's your main character? _____

_____

_____

_____

_____

✎ What's the setting? _____

_____

_____

_____

_____

✎ When does it take place—past, present, or future? _____

_____

_____

_____

_____

_____

✎ What are some of the obstacles the protagonist must overcome? _____

_____

_____

_____

_____

_____

✎ How does she or he overcome them?

_____

_____

_____

_____

_____

_____

Strange New World

Writers don't always rely on things they know about when they write. Sometimes they just make stuff up. Science fiction and fantasy authors often create completely new worlds or universes and fill them with out-of-this-world characters (most of whom, no matter how strange, have very human problems). Are you interested in creating a new world from your imagination? Try answering these questions to get you started:

✎ What kind of a world would you make? Would it be very different from ours?

✎ Where in the universe is this world? Is it orbiting a different star (or stars)?

_____

_____

_____

_____

_____

✎ What kinds of vegetation, if any, populate this world?

_____

_____

_____

_____

✎ What kinds of strange animals are there?

_____

_____

_____

_____

_____

✎ What are the people like? How do they act? What do they eat? How do they communicate? Are they technologically more advanced than us, or are they more like prehistoric humans?

_____

_____

_____

_____

_____

✐ What sort of magic, if any, exists? What is its source? If there's no magic, how will science play a role in this world? (Usually writers of science fiction try to imagine how today's technology and science will affect our future.)

_____

_____

_____

_____

_____

✐ Who are the good guys (your heroes)? _____

_____

_____

_____

_____

✐ Who are the bad guys (the characters trying to disrupt this world)?

_____

_____

_____

✐ What kind of government rules this world? A king or queen, a dictator or president, or somebody completely unexpected? _____

_____

_____

_____

_____

✐ What problem does this world have that will interest a reader?

_____

_____

_____

_____

Still-Stuck Busters

By now, you probably have an idea or two (or 200) brewing. The next few pages will give you hints on what comes next. But first, we've put together a list of what we like to call "still-stuck busters." The next time you're stuck for an idea, try one of these. They're pretty simple, fun, and 100-percent guaranteed to jump-start your poor idea-less brain.

- Read whatever you can get your hands on, and keep paper and pen close by in case an idea (or even a fragment of one) comes to you.

- Read advice columns in magazines and newspapers. Write your own answers to the questions, or create a character with some of the problems you read about.

- Keep a daily journal. Many writers keep journals, and it's a good way to practice writing every day. The best part about a journal is that no one else will ever read it, so you don't have to agonize over every word and constantly wonder, "Is this interesting?" Also, journals can be great sources of inspiration even years after they've been written. (So don't throw them away—even if you're embarrassed to look at them now.)

- Create characters or plots from the daily horoscopes. Pit a Libra against a Scorpio! Write what happens when a Taurus goes outside even though his horoscope told him to stay in bed.

- Keep a notebook and pen by your bed and write down any dreams you have as soon as you wake up.

- Solve the world's problems. (Don't just think it out; write it out.)

- Write a better ending for a book or movie you saw.

- Alter an old picture book. Rewrite the book so that it still makes sense with the pictures but tells a different story.

- Write down your earliest memories.

(more on the next page)

- Write about the life of a 20-dollar bill: how it changes hands, how it's spent over the course of a month or a year, and even how it ends up getting destroyed.

- Describe something you've seen that you'll never ever forget.

- Imagine that your dog just kindly informed you, in English, that it's well past her dinnertime.

- If you could choose one superpower, which would it be: invisibility or the ability to fly? Write about why you chose that superpower.

- What issues or topics do you feel strongly about? Write about them.

- Take random photos with a digital camera, put them on your computer, and make up stories about them.

- Read the newspaper or listen to the news. Pick one story (for example, a natural disaster, a car accident, a speech) and imagine you witnessed it. Write about it as if you were there.

- Interview a person from ancient history.

- Write about a modern-day kid lost in some past historic time.

- Write about current issues.

- Imagine you just spotted a celebrity at the CD store who the world thinks is dead.

- Read tabloid headlines while in the checkout line at the grocery store. Write the stories that explain them.

- Describe everything you know about your favorite person.

What!? You found an Idea!

Well, that's awesome. Pat yourself on the back. Now it's time to get writing. Here are some tips for getting that first draft written.

➠ Freewrite on your topic (see page 16).

➠ Create a web (see page 56).

➠ Think of your first draft as that nonstop conversation you have with your best friend on the first day of school after not seeing him or her for the whole summer. Don't think of your first draft as the term paper you have to hand in to your Language Arts teacher.

➠ No matter how bad you think your first draft is, don't stop writing and don't criticize it. It's called the FIRST draft for a reason. It's where you get all your ideas down on paper. It's not for anyone to read but you. Think of your first draft as the clay you'll use to sculpt your masterpiece. If you beat yourself up over your first draft, you'll probably never get to a second draft.

➠ Stop caring about how neatly you're writing, whether you're spelling everything correctly, and whether you've used the correct "there" (or is it "their" or "they're"?). If you know the correct punctuation or spelling, use it, but don't let constant worrying about that stuff stop you from the flow of your first draft.

➠ When you get stuck...read the next chapter!

Chapter 2

Are You Stuck?

YOU'VE GOT A GREAT IDEA, AND YOU'RE WRITING! In fact, you're on a roll.

Words effortlessly appear on the page, and you even say to yourself, "Hah, this writing stuff is easy." Then...like a car about to run out of gas, you sputter. The speedometer shows 40...30...20...10 miles per hour. The words come more and more slowly, until it becomes official. You're stuck. Desperation sets in, and you feel like tossing the whole project. Wait! Read this chapter first. Writers not only develop ways to find ideas for their writing, but they also figure out strategies for keeping themselves writing when the going gets tough.

Heeeeelp! MY hero is about to fall off a cliff, and I don't know how to save her!

Your First Getting Unstuck Tidbit

The going gets tough sooner or later for every writer out there.

Your Second Getting Unstuck Tidbit

Getting stuck doesn't mean you're kaput as a writer—it's not as hopeless as it feels.

Your Third Getting Unstuck Tidbit

Getting unstuck takes some effort. Most likely you won't get unstuck sitting at your desk waiting for your Muse (see page 53) to come and save you. You need to take charge and get yourself out of your writing rut. Check out this chapter and work on the activities. Remember the techniques that work, and start developing your own.

I have writer's block.

I don't know what to write next!

What's on tv?

I give up!

Your First Line of Attack

The first thing you should do when you're stuck is to get a drink of water. Don't drink too much of that sugary stuff. Sit down, and try again.

Here are some other simple things to try.

➤ Reread what you've already written. Read it twice if you need to. Circle parts you really like. You should also read it out loud. Nobody needs to listen, so go into a closet if you want. (Bring a flashlight.)

➤ Don't cross out too much. Remember that this is a first draft, which is for getting the words down on paper. You're creating the clay, not the sculpture.

➤ Make sure you're comfortable. Do you have good light? How's the seat you're sitting on? Change your setting to see whether that helps. Try writing upside down. Write in a beanbag chair. Find a different pen or pencil. Use a crayon.

➤ Shut out that inner voice that's telling you your writing stinks.

➤ Ask yourself whether you're writing about something you care about. If not, stop trying and find something else to write about.

➤ If you're writing a story, try writing a poem about the same subject.

➤ Are you trying to write a rhyming poem? Create a poem that doesn't rhyme.

➤ Horror got you down? Try mystery.

➤ Stop and try again tomorrow.

And no matter what those little voices in your head are trying to tell you, you're not wasting your time by doing any of these activities. You're giving your mind and imagination time to regroup—and you just might surprise yourself with some fresh ideas, words, concepts, and more.

Make a Muse

In Greek mythology, the Muses were nine sisters whose sole purpose in life was to inspire artists and help them create. Each Muse had a specialty. Artists made sacrifices to their specific Muses, so a love poet would revere the Muse Erato, while a comedian would venerate the Muse Thalia.

What kind of Muse do you need? What would she look like? Where would she come from? How would you find her and convince her you need her help?

Example Time

Name: Crossoutia
The Muse of: 1st Drafts
Origin: Created by mounds of crumpled up paper
Favorite thing: Sharpened pencils with brand new erasers
Pet peeve: Procrastination
How to invoke her: Lay all of your books, plus three newly sharpened pencils, on your desk. Call her name five times while spinning counterclockwise.

✎ **Now create your own muse.**

Name _____

The Muse of _____

Origin _____

Favorite thing _____

Pet peeve _____

How to invoke her _____

Doodle for Your Noodle

Doodling isn't just for boring class lectures anymore!

In fact, doodling can lead to unblocking your brain. So take a moment or two or three and doodle away right here. Think doodling is a waste of time? Well, scores of doodlers have doodled their way to fame and fortune, including Leonardo da Vinci, Charles Darwin, and Dr. Seuss.

Doodling has been scientifically proven to help explain ideas. It also relieves stress and frustration, and, well... hee hee ... it's fun.

Don't think too much about what you're drawing. Just draw. And don't worry about what your doodles look like.

Are You Stuck?

Untangle Your Writing

Webbing or clustering can help you get started writing, but it also works well to help untangle your thoughts, ideas, and story plots.

Here's a character web for a short story.

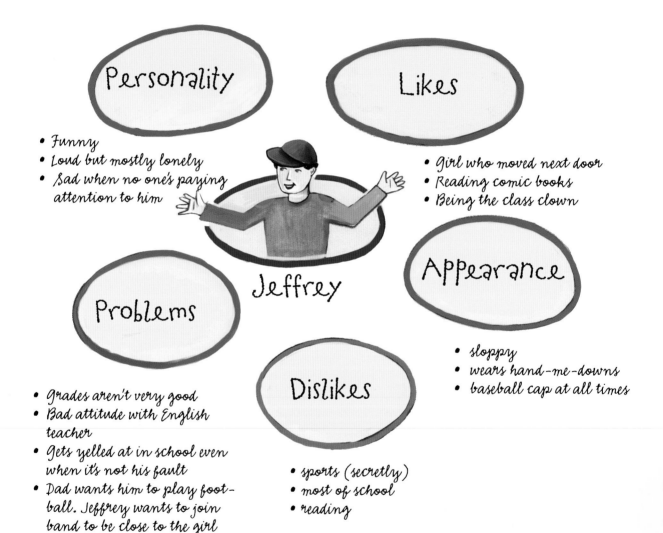

Personality
- Funny
- Loud but mostly lonely
- Sad when no one's paying attention to him

Likes
- Girl who moved next door
- Reading comic books
- Being the class clown

Jeffrey

Appearance
- sloppy
- wears hand-me-downs
- baseball cap at all times

Problems
- Grades aren't very good
- Bad attitude with English teacher
- Gets yelled at in school even when it's not his fault
- Dad wants him to play football. Jeffrey wants to join band to be close to the girl who just moved in next door.

Dislikes
- sports (secretly)
- most of school
- reading

This is a little like freewriting, except that you get to draw this cool web and you may be able to make some connections faster. You can then use the web as an outline to keep you going. Add to it each time you get stuck.

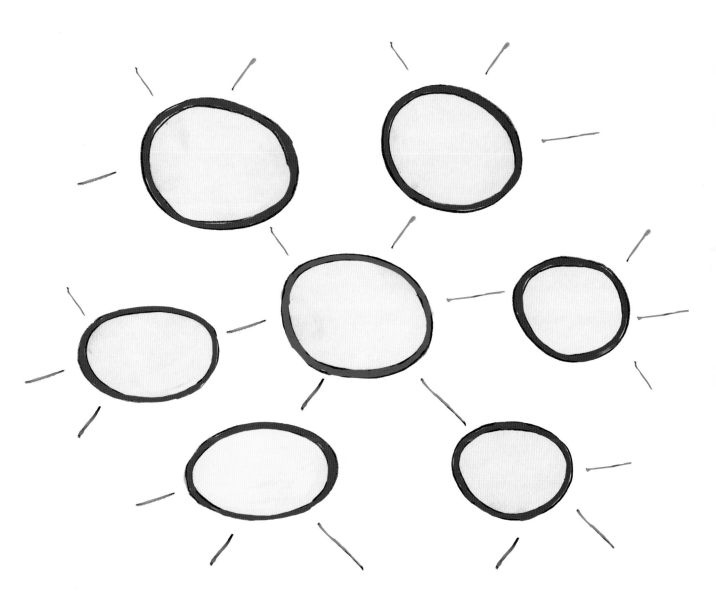

You can also use webbing to focus on particular points in a story that are bothering you. You can create a web for one or all of your characters or even for your story's setting.

Got Plot?

Plot: It's what happens in your story. A good story always has a good plot, and a good plot is almost always about a problem and how the main character goes about solving it. Not knowing what your characters are going to do next is one of the easiest ways to get stuck. Figuring out the plot will probably get you writing again.

A roller coaster ride is a lot like the plot of a story. You start out slow, pick up speed as you go uphill, and then have a wild ride down to the end.

CRISIS

This is the main conflict of your story. The crisis will change something about your main character.

When Jeffrey's friend Warren is accused of cheating on a math test, Warren says Julie gave him the answers. Jeffrey knows this is a lie, and he is torn between feelings of loyalty for his friend and wanting to make things right for Julie.

RISING ACTION

Something happens to complicate the life of your main character.

Jeffrey wants to impress Julie when he sees her at school, but she walks away from him when he makes fun of a younger student who turns out to be her brother.

INTRODUCTION

This part introduces the main character, setting, and problem.

Jeffrey, a bright yet often misunderstood 12-year-old student in a small town in Maine, is confused when Julie, the new girl next door, is nice to him, and he doesn't feel like making fun of her.

CLIMAX

Here, your main character deals with the crisis. This is the highest point in the action of your story. It's also known as the turning point, where everything changes for your main character, usually for the better.

Jeffrey is called to the principal's office while Warren cheers him on, knowing he will protect him. As Jeffrey sits outside the office, he feels really confused about what he's going to do. When called inside, he tells the principal the truth.

RESOLUTION

Now everything gets wrapped up. The readers see the change that happened in your main character because of the crisis.

Warren is suspended from school, and Jeffrey's supposed friends bully him on the bus ride home for ratting Warren out. As Jeffrey tries to get off the bus, one kid trips him, and his books fall all over the bus. As he picks up his books, he realizes that Julie has knelt down to help him. They both smile.

The end.

★ACTION★

Your Plot Roller Coaster (with a twist)

Here's your very own roller coaster to work out your story line. You don't have to list every moment in the story here. (You may not even know everything that's going to happen.) However, feel free to add other plot elements along this roller coaster. Include lots of struggle and character development.

RISING ACTION

_____

_____

_____

_____

_____

_____

Draw your main character here

INTRODUCTION

Main character _____

Setting _____

Problem _____

_____

_____

_____

_____

_____

CRISIS

See the list of different types of conflict on page 62 for ideas.

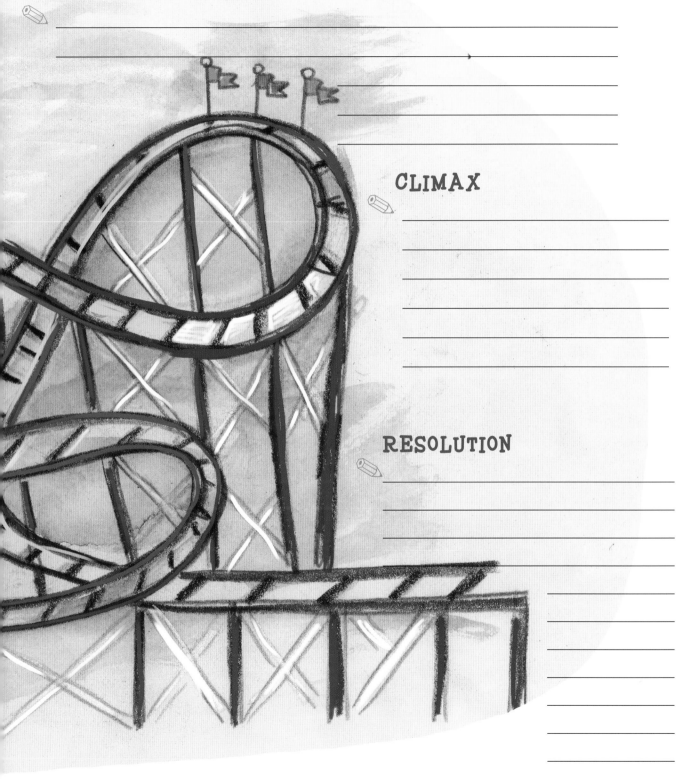

_____

_____

_____

_____

_____

CLIMAX

_____

_____

_____

_____

_____

_____

RESOLUTION

_____

_____

_____

_____

_____

_____

_____

_____

_____

Is Your Main Character Bored?

Maybe you have a great character and you're not sure what to have her do. There are several types of conflict used in fiction. You can have just one in your story, or you can have more than one. After each example below think of ways to involve your main character in that type of conflict.

Person vs. Person

Two people have different goals or convictions that bring them into conflict.

main character vs. school bully

_____

_____

_____

Person vs. Society

The main character is in conflict with the social order that surrounds her. For instance, your character could be in conflict with the school's popular crowd.

main character vs. her town's racism

_____

_____

_____

_____

Person vs. Self

Sometimes you're your own worst enemy. In this type of conflict, the main character struggles to overcome something about herself. You usually see this type of conflict as part of a larger story.

main character vs. low self-esteem

_____

_____

_____

_____

Person vs. Nature

The protagonist is in conflict with the environment or with animals. Often these are survival stories. Your character could be stuck in the Antarctic or lost in the subway of New York City, for example. He or she will have to figure out how to survive.

shipwrecked protagonist vs. desert island

_____

_____

_____

_____

_____

_____

Person vs. Fate

Destiny impels the main character toward some end, which he knows is coming and doesn't want to have happen. He tries to outwit fate.

main character vs. deadly illness

_____

_____

_____

_____

_____

_____

Whodunit? The Mysteries of Mystery Writing Revealed

A mystery is one of those pieces of writing where the author has to know how it all ends before she starts writing. So, to write your mystery, you have to work backward. Decide what your mystery is, and what the solution is. Think of something that is mysterious. It could be a news report you heard on the radio, or a question that keeps you up late at night.

✎ Write your mystery idea here.

_____

_____

_____

_____

_____

_____

✎ Now write a bunch of explanations for what might have happened. Don't just stick to logical explanations; get a little zany. These ideas will help you come up with tricky ways to throw your hero (and your reader) offtrack.

_____

_____

_____

_____

Are You Stuck?

You'll need some great characters for your mystery. Make sure your main character is a good, strong, interesting person, but not too perfect (see page 32 for Tragic Flaws). Make some of the other characters enigmatic (mysterious) or seemingly evil ("He's a bad guy; no, he's a good guy"). This will help create more mystery and suspense.

The Main Character

Name _____

Age _____

Occupation _____

Goal _____

Weakness _____

The Suspects

Name _____   Name _____

Age _____   Age _____

Occupation _____   Occupation _____

Goal _____   Goal _____

Weakness _____   Weakness _____

The Bad Guy

Name _____

Age _____

Occupation _____

Goal _____

Weakness _____

✎ List clues for your characters to discover. If you'd like, write down how the characters react to the clues as well.

_____

_____

_____

_____

_____

✎ Foreshadowing is what happens when you give your readers clues that you don't reveal to your main character. For instance, your hero's little brother states his hatred for pickles on page 2. Later, preferably at a climactic moment in the story, the little brother has to eat pickles to escape from an evil clown. List some foreshadowing possibilities.

_____

_____

✎ The red herring is a special term for fake clues that you give readers to throw them off track. Red herrings are great, because they keep readers guessing until the very end. But be careful to give readers more real clues than false ones. List some possible red herring clues.

_____

_____

✎ Suspense is always good in a mystery. Write a list of suspenseful words, places, sounds, and activities. Refer back to this list as you write your story.

_____

_____

✎ Surprise! Everybody loves surprises...especially in a mystery. Surprise your readers every now and again by having something unexpected happen to your characters. This will keep your readers guessing. Write a list of things that might surprise your characters.

_____

_____

✎ The setting is a very important aspect of your story. You can use it to create a sense of eeriness. Write down some creepy places, such as the locker room at night, and describe them using all five senses (see page 95).

_____

_____

_____

Main Character at the Wheel

Do you have a main character but are not sure what he'll do next? Set up an interview with him. Learning more about the character can help get your story moving again. The idea is to ask questions that will get your character to reveal more about himself beyond what you already know. Write the answers in your main character's voice, using the words and phrases he would use. (You can do this exercise for all your characters.)

Describe where and how you wake up every day.

What do you eat for breakfast?

Describe the clothes you wear most often.

If you knew you'd be away from home for three months, what three people or things would you want to take with you?

What annoys you?

✎ What makes you happy? _____

_____

_____

✎ What's your proudest moment? _____

_____

✎ Describe the most frightening or nerve-wracking thing you've ever seen, done, or thought about. _____

_____

_____

✎ If you saw a dog get hit by a car, what would you do?

_____

_____

_____

✎ If you saw someone stealing, what would you do? _____

_____

_____

_____

✎ What would you never, ever do? _____

_____

_____

✎ Who can you talk to about anything and everything (share your secrets and problems, etc.)?

_____

_____

_____

✎ What are your best qualities? _____

_____

✎ If you could change anything about yourself, what would it be?

_____

_____

✎ What do people think you are like?

_____

_____

✎ Describe what you think your life will be like in five years.

_____

_____

✎ What do you think is going to happen in the story?

_____

_____

✎ What do you want to do next in the story?

_____

_____

✎ What do you like about the story? What do you dislike?

_____

_____

_____

Are You Stuck?   69

A Secret Dialogue

Sometimes to get unstuck you need to see your story from a whole different perspective. Looking at your story through two different characters' eyes is a great way to discover new things about your story—especially if those two characters are talking to each other.

For this exercise, you can either use two characters who are already in your story or create two entirely new characters. Pick two minor characters who are very different from each other. Put them in a room together and start them talking. Make sure they stay in character the entire time.

Have them retell the entire story to each other. Begin their conversation with what has happened so far. Don't just retell the story from one perspective and then the other, though. Make the two characters talk it out. As they talk to each other, let them reveal how they feel about what has happened.

The characters can also share their reflections on what other characters are like, and speculate about their relationships.

Once you have a good dialogue going, let the conversation move on to what they think will happen next.

If you don't want to use two characters from your story, you can make up two entirely different characters. Don't worry about writing them into your story later. They're just here for this activity. Make sure the two characters are very different. For instance, one of them could be harshly critical of the story, while the other loves everything about it.

Says Who?

Another way to get unstuck is to switch your story's point of view. Your narrator (the voice that tells the story) has three very different ways he or she can recount events, and you can gain some insight by exploring them.

First Person

First person uses "I" statements to describe events, feelings, and thoughts. For example:

I could feel the stares of everyone on the bus as I tried to pick up my books. The tears welled up in my eyes till I could barely see, but I could feel someone next to me, helping. It was Julie. I felt a smile come to my lips as I tried to think of a joke, but all that came out of my mouth was, "Thanks."

Your first person can be the main character, a witness, or a reteller of the story. This is a limiting point of view because the author stays right inside the character's head and never comes out. That means the reader has to rely only on what that character believes he sees, and the character doesn't see himself.

Second Person

Second person uses "you" statements directed at the reader. Second person either makes the reader part of the book or pretends to be talking to one person in particular. It's not used often. Here's an example of this technique:

You can feel the stares of everyone on the bus as you try to pick up your books. It's all you can do to keep from crying. When Julie comes over to help you, she smiles. You try to think of a joke, but all that comes out of your mouth is, "Thanks."

Third Person

Third person tells the story using "he," "she," and "it" to describe the actions of characters. Here's an example of an omniscient (all-knowing) narrator sharing the thoughts of any character in a story whenever the writer wants:

Jeffrey could feel the stares of everyone on the bus as he tried to pick up the books. Shame burned his cheeks as tears welled up in his eyes, making it impossible to see who was next to him. Julie felt sad to see Jeffrey in such a bad way, but also a little satisfied realizing that he now knew how the people he used to tease felt. Seeing his tears quickly erased any feelings of satisfaction, though. Jeffrey could feel a smile come to his lips as he tried to think of a joke, but all that came out of his mouth was, "Thanks."

A limited third person can share the thoughts of just one character or one character at a time (such as focusing on only one protagonist in each chapter). An objective (fact-based) third person can't get inside the heads of characters but can tell exactly what is said and done.

Now choose a different point of view for your story and try rewriting parts of it here. In other words, if you're inside your main character's head (first person), get out and try an omniscient third person approach.

WRITING HORROR STORIES

A horror story is just like any other kind of story, except for one thing: the horror. Horror is a whole lot more than blood and gore—you want to disturb your reader's deepest, darkest emotions. To pump up your horror story, check out these special tips and tricks.

Killer Characters

Your characters can't just exist to get eaten, disintegrated, or murdered by the bad guy. The reader has to care about what happens to the characters. The more strongly your readers can identify with one or more of your characters, the easier it will be to scare your readers.

What Was That Noise?

Sounds are very important in horror stories. Creaking stairs, ominous footsteps, cracking branches, weird scratching noises, and piercing screams will heighten the suspense and tension.

Pick Up the Pace

Horror stories move quickly because you want to build as much tension and suspense as possible. There are two easy ways to do this. The first is to use a cliffhanger to end a chapter, and then pick up your story in a different place with a different character. The second is to shorten your sentences in key horror scenes. This will make them read faster, adding to the dramatic tension.

Suspense

Build up the suspense before the conflict or crisis occurs by putting little details in that at first seem insignificant but get scarier and scarier as the story progresses. For instance, if your character is going to be attacked by the boogeyman that lives in the basement at the end of the story, start off with odd noises coming from there. As the story progresses, make the noises happen more and more frequently as your characters come closer to figuring out what's making the noise.

The Gore

Go for emotional and psychological disturbance, not just the pure gross-out factor. Here's a good test. Check out your disturbing paragraphs. Can you take them out of the story without changing the story significantly? Make sure that the horror has a reason for existing. It will have a stronger effect on the reader if it is tied to plot or character development.

The End

Leave a loose thread in the end. Some horror stories have happy endings, but not many. Usually the very last sentence, after the surviving heroes think they're safe, reveals a still lurking danger.

✎ **Write down ideas for your horror story.** _____

_____

_____

_____

_____

_____

_____

_____

_____

_____

Lights, Camera, Storyboard!

Before the cameras start rolling, movie directors often draw sketches of each camera angle of every scene in the movie. This shows the camera crew, actors, and everyone else how the script will translate onto film. This sort of comic book version of a movie is called a storyboard, and it's the director's vision of what the film will look like. You can make a storyboard of almost any kind of writing to see whether you're happy with the action, to help you organize the plot, and especially to help you decide what should happen next. If you need more boxes, make your own storyboard sheets.

Are You Stuck?

Are You Stuck?

Mr. Not-So-Scary Writing Teacher to the Rescue

Sometimes you need a professional to get you out of your writing jam. If we had a toll-free number, we'd love to provide that service. But, we have writing to do. So, we are happy to introduce you to Mr. Not-So-Scary Writing Teacher. His job is to ask you questions to help you get out of a funk. Sometimes it's good to talk about (or, in this case, write about) the status of your writing. Mr. Not-So Scary Writing Teacher asks good questions, and he always likes your answers.

✎ So, tell me about what you're working on.

_____

_____

_____

_____

_____

_____

✎ How's it going so far?

_____

_____

_____

_____

_____

_____

✏️ What problems have you found so far? _____

_____

_____

_____

_____

✏️ What in your writing has surprised you? _____

_____

_____

_____

_____

_____

✏️ Why do you think you're stuck? _____

_____

_____

_____

_____

✏️ What will you work on next? _____

_____

_____

_____

Mr. Not-So-Scary Writing Teacher's Do's and Don'ts for Getting Unstuck:

☛ Don't rip pages out of your notebook and crumple them up. In fact, many writers never throw away anything. Some writing you thought stunk six months ago might lead to your masterpiece tomorrow.

☛ If you're stuck because it's difficult, keep working. If you're stuck because you're bored, consider a new topic. Yes, starting over can be a daunting task, but it's better than writing something you no longer care about.

Chapter 3

Getting Better All the Time

YOU'VE GOT A FIRST DRAFT IN FRONT OF YOU.

It has a beginning, a middle, and an end. Maybe it's sloppy. Perhaps it's difficult to read. In some places, it may not even make sense. Guess what? It's perfect.

My first draft stinks. Somebody, help!

If writing your first draft is like speeding down the highway in a super-charged racecar, revising it is like traveling the same highway on foot. Along the way, you're picking up the trash and noticing the landscape. Revising your first draft means reading and rereading, cutting and adding, moving and shaking, and whatever else needs to be done to get it ready for your audience. In other words, writing **IS** revising, and this step is just as important as finding an idea and getting the words down.

I don't know how to revise my writing.

First Important Revising Step

Take a break. Try not to revise your first draft the same day you finish it. Give your brain a rest.

84

Second Important Revising Step

If you're suffering from First Draftitis (see page 8), read your first draft out loud. That should cure you.

Third Important Revising Step

Take as long as you need. You may have to put it away for a week or even a month. Don't feel that you have to rush through your revisions.

Fourth Important Revising Step

Save each draft of your writing and put the date you worked on it somewhere on the draft. This can help tremendously, especially if you decide you liked an earlier version of your piece better.

Fifth Important Revising Step

Read this chapter. In it, you'll be able to take chunks of your draft and strengthen your plot, character development, dialogue, word choice, punctuation, usage, spelling, and more.

Note: Revising is not proofreading. Proofreading is what you do after you're finished thinking about your writing. It's fixing your spelling, punctuation, and sentence structure. The best way to learn that stuff is to keep writing and check out the proofreading section at the end of this chapter.

Cut and Tape

Grab a pair of scissors and some tape, and get ready to reorganize your manuscript. You're probably used to cutting and pasting pieces of your writing in word processing programs on your computer, but the old-fashioned version of those tools are great for editing your manuscript.

Step 1: Photocopy or scan your first draft. Make sure you only have writing on one side of each page.

Step 2: Start cutting. The best place to cut is between paragraphs. Cut your paragraphs into smaller segments if you need to.

Step 4: Arrange and rearrange your writing in different ways. Changing the order of ideas can really shake things up. Maybe your last paragraph makes a good first paragraph. Maybe your story reads better with the first paragraph out of the way entirely. Cutting and rearranging can help you get your time-line straight and help you decide where you want to put everything.

As you move stuff around, try to spot problems, holes, and lack of transitions between paragraphs.

Step 5: If you want to add new text, place a star where you want to add it, and write the text on a new piece of paper with a star on it, so you know where it goes.

Step 7: Don't tape down anything until you feel pretty confident that your new order is better.

You can use this technique with poetry, essays, personal narratives, and just about any kind of writing you're doing. And even if you use a computer to write your first drafts, print your draft and cut away.

Editing Marks

Here are some editing tools you can use as you mark up your manuscript.

Insert

Good
writing is writing that Works really Well writing is Reviising.

Move

Good writing is writing that Works really Well writing is Reviising.

Delete

writing is Reviising. Good writing is writing that Works really Well

Delete & close up

writing is Reviising. Good writing is writing that Works

Capitalize

writing is Revising. Good writing is writing that Works

Lowercase

Writing is Revising. Good writing is writing that Works

New paragraph

Writing is revising. Good writing is writing that works

Insert period

Writing is revising.

Good writing is writing that works

Oops, I changed my mind.

Writing is revising.

stet
Good writing is writing that works.

On the Operating Table

It's time to operate on your first draft. One strong approach to revising is to reread your manuscript several times, each time looking for something different to fix. The first step is to rewrite your first draft on the following blank pages.

Here are some tips to make revising and editing your manuscript easier:

🔖 Double-space your draft. In other words, skip a line as you write. This leaves room for adding text to your manuscript.

🔖 Feel free to add changes that come up as you rewrite.

🔖 Write legibly.

🔖 Write in paragraphs.

🔖 Save all your drafts in a folder and date them so you know which draft is most recent.

🔖 Don't be afraid to cross out stuff, but use a single line. If you scribble out the whole thing, you may want to go back and reread it, and you won't be able to.

🔖 If you're writing on a computer, simply print your first draft and glue it to these pages. Don't forget to double space the document. If you want to do all your editing on the computer, save each draft under a different name. Also, print your different drafts in case your computer decides to take a permanent vacation.

Getting Better All the Time

_____

_____

_____

_____

_____

_____

_____

_____

_____

_____

_____

_____

_____

_____

_____

_____

_____

_____

_____

_____

Okay, your draft is here and ready to work on. Save your old draft just in case, and simply read the rest of the chapter and follow the instructions.

"Don't Say the Old Lady Screamed. Bring Her On and Let Her Scream."

What this famous quote by Mark Twain means is that it's almost always better to show what's happening in your story, narrative, or poem than it is simply to tell it.

AAAARGGGHHH!

So instead of
"The old lady screamed."

You write
"Aaaarrrrrgggghhhh!"

Here's another example:

Tell: The car sounded weird on the way to school.

Show: The car clanked and roared as it limped toward school.

Read your manuscript and circle places where you think you're telling rather than showing. You can try to revise them right there, or you can rewrite several of them here and play with them.

✎ **Original description** _____

_____

_____

✎ **Show it** _____

_____

_____

✎ **Original description** _____

_____

_____

✎ **Show it** _____

_____

_____

✎ **Original description** _____

_____

_____

✎ **Show it** _____

_____

_____

✎ **Original description** _____

_____

_____

✎ **Show it** _____

_____

_____

✎ **Original description** _____

_____

_____

✎ **Show it** _____

_____

_____

✎ **Original description** _____

_____

_____

✎ **Show it** _____

_____

The Amazing "So What?" "What Else?" Revising Method

This method can be used throughout your revision stage. It's rather simple. Here are the steps:

Step 1: Read your manuscript with a different colored pen in hand.

Step 2: As you read, look at your descriptions, dialogue, and other places where you provide detail. Circle them.

Step 3: After reading the manuscript, return to the circled items and apply the question, "So what?" to them. If you can answer the question, then it's important to the story. If you can't, cut it.

Step 4: Then ask "What else?" Can you think of other details that could help your writing be more precise?

Example Time

Check out this sentence:

Jeffrey laced up his battered high-tops.

This is a description that you would have circled in your manuscript.

So what?

Well, describing his sneakers as "battered" shows that his family doesn't have money to buy new shoes. This also leads to tension later in the story when he realizes he really likes his next-door neighbor, who is nice but whose family has more money.

What else?

His shoelace could break, making Jeffrey's day even more frustrating. If you had simply written, "Jeffrey put on his shoes," would you have an answer for "So what?" Not unless it was the first time he put shoes on in eight years!

Sensory Details

Animate your writing with all the sights, sounds, smells, and sensations of life. All you need to do is use the five senses to tell the story.

Look at the descriptions in your manuscript that you circled in the last activity. Do most of them rely on sight? Sight description is fine, but don't rely only on this sense to tell your story.

SOUND

Sound is the easiest sense (after sight) to put into your story. There are sounds all around you: ringing telephones, knocked-upon doors, footsteps, birdsongs, music, your own breath, and more. Put sounds in your story to let your readers hear what's happening at the same time your characters do.

She walked into an empty house.

Or

The floorboards creaked and the sound echoed through the rooms as she stepped into the house.

Try this one:

He dropped the carton of eggs on the sidewalk.

TOUCH

You can feel textures, heat, and cold. Remember, you don't just feel things with your hands, either. Every tiny piece of skin on your body is a touch receptor.

The tables in the school cafeteria haven't been cleaned in years.

Or

If you accidentally lean on the tables in the cafeteria, your elbows will get coated with the slick grease that has built up for years.

Practice describing touch.

Get a branch from a tree. Touch it. Describe how the branch feels in as many different ways as you can. (Don't use the word "tree," "branch," or "bark.")

 _____

_____

_____

_____

TASTE

Mmmm...taste is a good sense. Remember that you taste things other than food. The air in an old, musty building tastes a lot different than the air in a field full of flowers.

He quickly ate his strawberry ice cream.

Or

As soon as the first taste of cool, creamy strawberry ice cream melted on his tongue, he went insane.

Practice describing taste.

Eat an orange. Describe what it tastes like in as many different ways as you can. (Don't use the words "orange" or "citrus.")

 _____

_____

_____

_____

SMELL

The sense of smell is one of the least-used senses in writing. That means that when you put a powerful smell description in your story, it's like socking your reader in the nose!

It was going to rain.

Or

The air was heavy with the earthy scent of rain.

Practice describing smell.

Get some flowers. Put them into a vase. Describe how they smell. (Don't use the words "flower" or "perfume.")

✎ _____

_____

_____

_____

_____

_____

_____

_____

_____

Here are some other things to keep in mind:

➥ Don't cram all your sensory details into one paragraph. You'll give your readers sensory overload! Spread them throughout the story. Be careful, though; if your manuscript is too full of descriptions, readers will start to wonder whether anything actually happens in the story.

➥ A good rule of thumb is to save sensory details for things that are essential to your plot, character development, or setting. If you find yourself sticking gorgeous sunsets at the end of every chapter, just because you really like sunsets, cut them.

Figurative Language

Figurative language is wording that knocks your reader upside the head: It's real, it makes a point, and it rings in your ears. Figurative language gives your writing depth and drama without adding lengthy sentences.

Metaphor: This is a word or phrase that ordinarily means one thing but is used to mean something else, thus making a comparison. "It's a puzzle," "a sea of troubles," and "all the world's a stage" are metaphors.

✎ Turn some descriptions in your story into metaphors.

_____

_____

_____

_____

Simile: A simile is when two different things are combined with the word "like" or "as." For instance, "he walks like a duck" and "the sun was as red as a tomato" are both similes.

✎ Turn some descriptions in your story into similes.

_____

_____

_____

_____

The difference between metaphor and simile can be a little tricky. Look for the words "like" or "as." They indicate a simile. "Her eyes were like emeralds" is a simile. "Her eyes were emeralds" is a metaphor.

Personification: This means giving human emotions or attributes to animals and objects. "The stars are jealous of your brilliance" is an example of personification. (Stars can't actually be jealous.)

✎ Write some personifications. _____

_____

_____

_____

_____

Kenning: This is when a more descriptive word (or words) is used in place of a noun. For instance, instead of calling it "the school cafeteria" you could call it "the place where greasy, cold food goes to die" or "the place of bellyaches."

✎ Write some kennings. _____

_____

_____

_____

_____

Hyperbole: This is the fancy literary term for exaggeration. For instance, "I'm so hungry I could eat a horse" is a hyperbole (and a cliché as well).

✎ Write some hyperboles. _____

_____

_____

_____

_____

Read through your first draft with a pencil in your hands. Circle places that could be improved, strengthened, and condensed by using figurative language.

Get Inside the Heart and Mind of Your Main Character

Once you've figured out your main character, you can communicate some of that information (whatever's useful to your story) to your readers. Read your draft. Put ellipses (...) at every point in your draft where you think your reader needs to know what the main character or narrator is thinking and feeling. Then go back and add reflections.

Here are some ways to incorporate the answers you just came up with into your story:

Flashback: This brings your readers back in time so they can see an important moment in your protagonist's life. A flashback to the scariest moment in your main character's life would be a great way to show readers what happened.

Write a **flashback**. _____

_____

_____

_____

_____

_____

_____

_____

_____

_____

_____

_____

_____

_____

Interior monologue: This describes what your character is thinking. It's a great way to let the reader know things about the character that he wouldn't want other characters to know, such as what annoys him or what he thinks he'll be doing in five years.

✏ Write an **interior monologue**.

_____

_____

_____

_____

_____

_____

_____

_____

_____

_____

_____

_____

_____

_____

Anecdote: An anecdote is a short, sweet, and funny story about an event that's useful to the story. Either your protagonist or a character close to your protagonist can tell an anecdote. This is a great way to use your answer to the question "What was the proudest moment of your life?" on page 68.

✏️ Write an **anecdote**. _____

_____

_____

_____

_____

_____

_____

_____

Dialogue: This is a conversation between two or more characters. What your character says and how she says it will tell your readers a lot about her. The other character's response will show your reader what other people think your protagonist is like.

✏️ Write **dialogue.** _____

_____

_____

_____

_____

_____

_____

_____

_____

Better Dialogue

Your dialogue will put your reader to sleep faster than you can write "she said" if you break some of the cardinal rules of good dialogue.

"And then he said, and then she said, and then he said, then she said like..., and then he goes... and then she jumped all crazy-like and said totally like..."

Like, wow.

1. Repetition: Don't have your characters tell each other something that readers already know. Skip it. And don't have them repeat back to each other what the last person said. That's lame.

2. Name calling: In real life, people don't address each other by name every other word. Don't make your characters do that unless there's a really good reason for it. (For instance, if there are several people in one scene, and a comment is directed at only one of them.)

3. Irrelevance: Make sure what your characters are saying has something to do with the story. It should relate to the plot, setting, or character development. Don't just let your characters blather on and on about nothing. Make them keep their mouths shut if they don't have anything good to contribute to a conversation.

4. Slowness: If you can show it faster or better with narration, do so.

5. Confusion: Use a tag line ("he said") every five or six interchanges to make sure your reader can understand who's talking.

Get Active

When the subject of a verb performs the action, the verb is in the active voice.

The pirate shoved the captain off the plank.

subject   action

When the subject receives the action, the verb is in the passive voice.

The captain was shoved off the plank by the pirate.

When possible, it is best to keep your sentences in the active voice. One way is to try to avoid using "is," "am," "are," "was," and "were" (the forms of "be").

Step 1: Circle every instance where you used forms of "be" in your draft.

Step 2: Write 10 of these examples.

_____

_____

_____

_____

_____

_____

_____

_____

_____

Step 3: Find the subject of the sentences so you can get rid of the passive voice.

_____

_____

_____

_____

_____

_____

_____

_____

_____

Example Time

Old: The car was parked by Stanley.

New and Improved: Stanley parked the car.

Old: The announcement to cancel the field trip was made by the teacher.

New and Improved: The teacher made the announcement to cancel the field trip.

Even Better: "I cancelled the field trip," said the teacher.

Take One Last Look Around

Thanks to your revisions, your writing is cleaner and clearer, and it tells your story better. Now's the time to take one last look at your manuscript before you proofread it.

🔌 Check your paragraphs: Do the very long ones need to be broken up? Your reader will assume that everything in a paragraph belongs together. If that's not true, split the paragraph.

🔌 Check your sentence length: Good paragraphs often have sentences with varying lengths. If a paragraph is full of simple, short sentences, try linking some of them to create a complex sentence.

🔌 Check the tense of your writing: Make sure that if you're writing in the past tense you don't suddenly switch to the present tense.

🔌 Make sure your lead grabs the reader: Read the introduction on page 6 again. Use dialogue, vivid description, or a jolting sentence to start your piece. This will make your readers want to continue.

🔌 Avoid clichés; they're boring: Get rid of sayings people have heard over and over again. Free as a bird? Boring. Big as a house? Boring.

🔌 Check your verb and subject agreement: The subject and verb of each sentence must agree in number. So if you use a singular subject (Henry), make sure you use a singular verb (eats). Henry and Jeffrey eat.

HEY!

write your awesome lead here

THE PROOFREADING PLAN

As we said before, proofreading is what you do to make sure your writing looks professional and is easier to read and enjoy. Writers proofread so their readers will not only understand their writing but will also spend their time reading instead of noticing their mistakes.

We could teach you about punctuation, spelling, and usage until the cows come home. (Sorry, we love this cliché.) But we won't. It's difficult to learn all these rules from a book, especially when you're trying to learn the stuff out of context. In other words, it's easier to learn about semicolons when you're trying to use one in your writing.

But you can use this book to become a better proofreader. This isn't an overnight success kind of promise but a "the-more-you-write-the-better-you'll-proofread" kind of promise.

Proofing Part 1: SPELLING

Step 1: Read your manuscript one last time. Circle any word that you're not 100 percent sure how to spell.

Step 2: Look up all the words at the same time.

Step 3: If some of the words you looked up are ones you use frequently, write down the correct spellings here. Keep adding to the list, and refer to it when proofing any piece of writing. You'll soon have a substantial list of words at your fingertips. You'll notice that these words will be spelled correctly more often than not the next time you use them.

Getting Better All the Time

Proofing Part 2: PUNCTUATION

Here's a secret. You don't need to know every punctuation rule ever invented. In fact, you know a bunch of them already. Periods aren't much of a problem. Question marks? You've got them covered. It's those pesky semicolons, commas, dashes, and colons that get you. So, what's a writer to do? Worry about only the stuff that trips you up in your own writing. In fact, you may never remember the difference between a semicolon and a comma until you use them a lot. Then, suddenly, they matter.

Use the cards on pages 111 to 114 to create your own deck of punctuation rules that you use and abuse. The first one is done for you.

Example Time

SEMICOLON

;

How it's used:

• To separate two closely related independent clauses (complete sentences)

• To separate items in a list that have commas in them already

Front

Examples

• She was a natural ballplayer; she could hit the ball a mile.

• Trenton, NJ; Fairfield, CT; and Norfolk, VA

Back

Proofing Part 3: OTHER COMMON MISTAKES

Not sure whether to use "there," "they're," or "their"? Create a card!

Is it okay to start off a sentence using a number? Create a card!

Is it "alright" or "all right"? You know what to do!

The best way to collect these little rules is to have a writer or a teacher proofread your manuscript. He or she will correct your problems, and then you can write the rules on cards so you can easily refer to them while you proofread. The more you write, the more cards you create.

Example Time

already
or
all ready

Already is an adverb that tells when.

All ready is a phrase meaning "completely ready."

Front

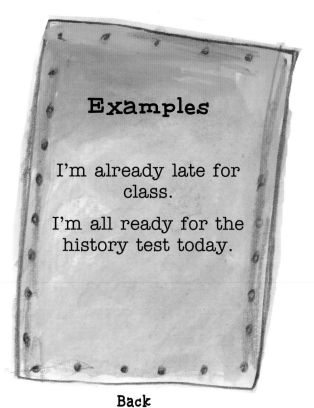

Examples

I'm already late for class.

I'm all ready for the history test today.

Back

Start your proofreading cards right here. Cut them out, collect them, and trade them with your friends. Make more cards when you need them.

Fronts

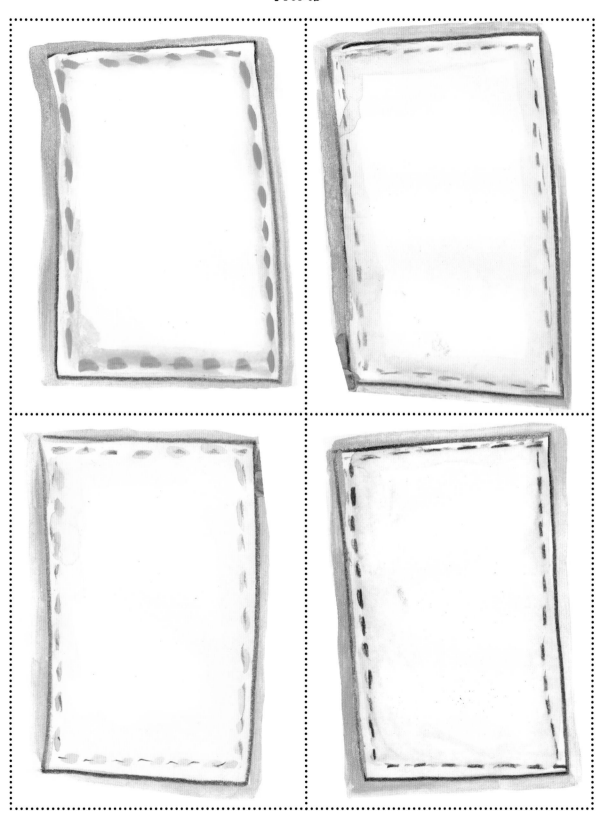

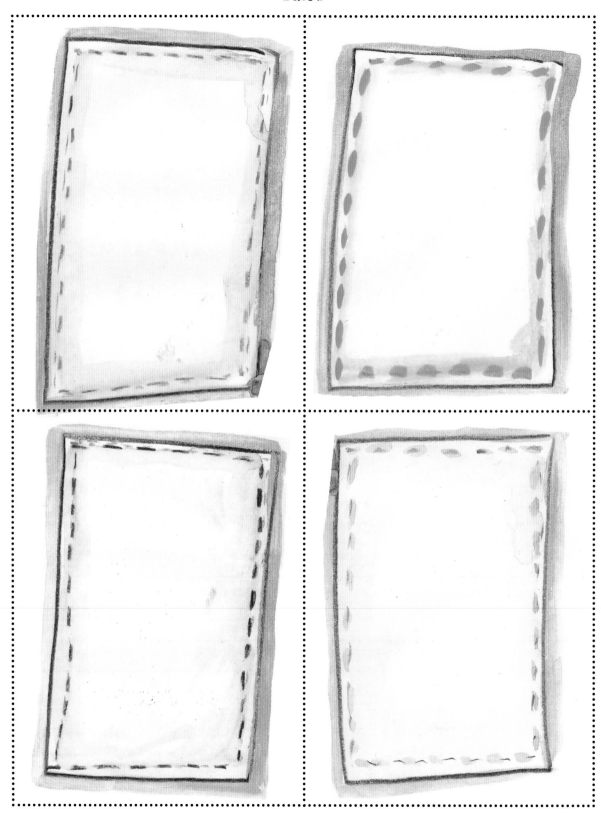

Getting Better All the Time

Fronts

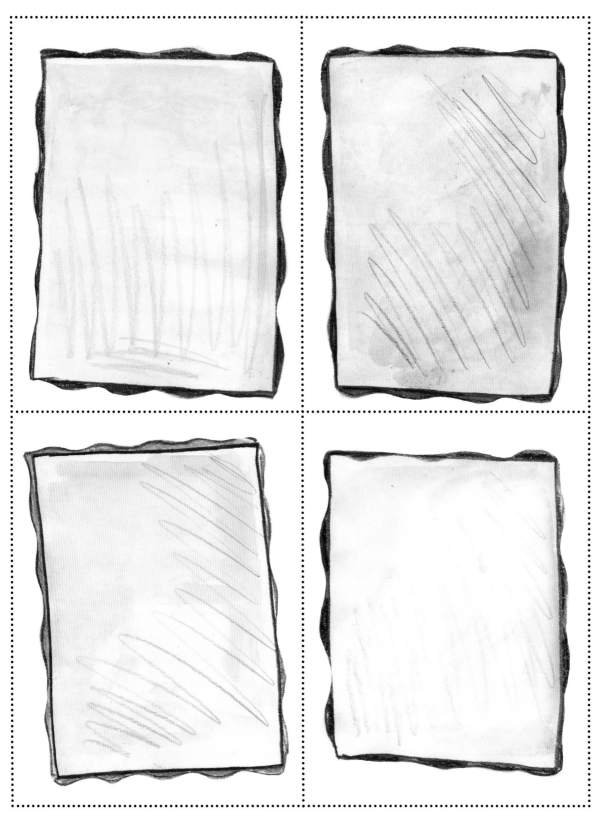

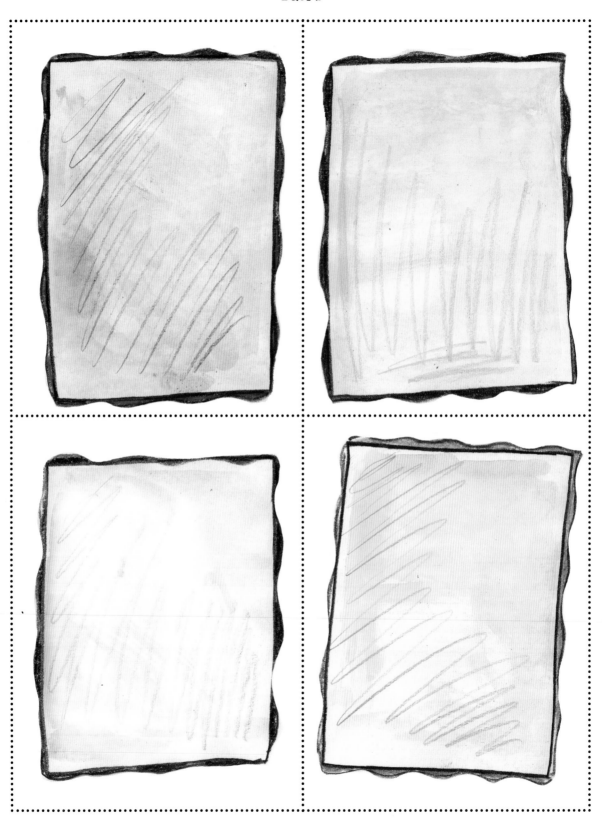

Getting Better All the Time

Get Some Feedback

Writers usually make friends with other writers. Not only can they sit around and talk about their fancy new computers or pens, but they can also bounce ideas off each other. They can ask for advice, get feedback on a manuscript they're working on, and try out a finished piece on an audience before publishing it. Now, you can get feedback from your mom, but since she thinks you're the next William Shakespeare, you may not get much good advice. If you don't have any writer friends yet, the best way to find some is to start a writer's group.

A writer's group is a bunch of writers who meet a few times each month to share their thoughts on each other's writing and to offer encouragement, ideas, and advice on becoming better writers.

Step 1: Create a list of possible kids who might be interested. Ask your teachers for candidates. Post a notice on a bulletin board at school.

INTERESTED KIDS	NUMBER	E-MAIL

Step 2: Contact the people on your list and sell them the idea of a writer's group. Here are some selling points:

➥ A writer's group is a great way to get strong, positive feedback for your writing.

➥ You'll get to see what other writers are doing, and that might challenge you to try something different.

➥ You'll get the opportunity to discuss the strong points of your writing, as well as the parts that need work.

➥ A writer's group is a great motivator to write more and better.

Step 3: Plan your first writer's group meeting. You really only need one other member. If you get 25 responses, you may have to suggest more than one group.

Date _____ Time _____ Location _____

Who's coming _____

_____

_____

_____

_____

Step 4: Conduct the first meeting. This is a get-acquainted meeting where you get to know each other a bit, talk about what you like to write and read, and decide how the writer's group will work. Make sure each member brings one piece of finished writing he or she wants to read to the group, along with enough copies of that piece for the rest of the group.

Weekly meeting time _____

Meeting running time _____

Person in charge _____

Snack person (Yes, snacks are important!) _____

_____

Step 5: Explain how the writer's group will work, and ask for suggestions. Here's one way to run a typical meeting:

🔹 Each member should read the manuscripts that were handed out at the end of the previous meeting.

🔹 Before the next meeting, members should write comments on each writing piece.

🔹 At the next meeting, a writer should read his work, while the others read along silently. Then, have each member comment on the piece. Have members first start off with something positive about the piece. Then, kindly mention something that needs work. It's also important that no one in the group makes fun of somebody and/or his writing.

🔹 While the readers are making their comments, the writer should not speak until everyone has commented. Remember, you're not there to critique each other as human beings. You're trying to help each other become better writers. Get an adult to moderate the meeting if the group is having trouble with this.

🔹 After all comments have been given, each member should hand the marked-up copy of the piece of writing to the reader. Then the next person reads, and you follow the same routine. Make sure someone keeps track of the time so that everyone has a chance to read and hear comments.

Questions to Ask Yourself While Reading Someone's Work

🔹 What works for you? Why?

🔹 What doesn't work? Why not?

🔹 What parts confuse you?

🔹 What sounds interesting to you?

🔹 What would you like to read more about?

🔹 What supportive comments can you add?

🔹 What ideas do you have regarding this piece?

GET YOUR WORDS OUT THERE

Real writing has real readers. You found a great idea, wrote a first draft, revised and rewrote it, edited and proofread it. It's time to publish your work. Here are some different ways to do it.

🖊 First, if you haven't done so already, type your final draft using a word processing program on a computer. If you don't have one at home, ask to use one at school.

🖊 Print or photocopy extra copies of your final draft and hand them out to family and friends.

🖊 Submit your piece to a local newspaper, a kid-friendly magazine, or even a book publisher. Make sure the sources you find actually publish kids' writing. Otherwise, you're wasting postage.

🖊 Submit your piece to writing contests. Have a teacher help you find a reputable competition. Some are scams!

🖊 Read **In Print: 40 Cool Publishing Projects for Kids** by Joe Rhatigan (Lark Books). There are lots of cool ideas in this book for getting your words out there.

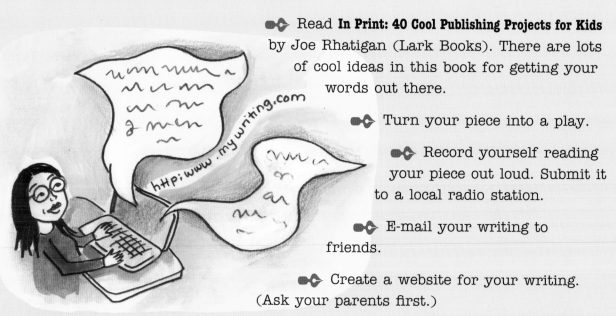

🖊 Turn your piece into a play.

🖊 Record yourself reading your piece out loud. Submit it to a local radio station.

🖊 E-mail your writing to friends.

🖊 Create a website for your writing. (Ask your parents first.)

🖊 Have an open mic night where you and some friends read your finished writing to each other.

🖊 Go to a copy center and explore the different ways you can bind your writing. You may even be able to create your own book.

You're at the End of the Book. Now What?

Keep writing. Go back to the beginning of this book and start all over again. If the book is all filled up, buy another one. Or get a notebook and make it your official writer's notebook. Re-create your spelling list. Write down your dreams and silly thoughts. Tape fortunes from cookies to the pages. Doodle. Keep it close by so you won't miss anything.

Our Last Words

Writing isn't about being some sort of genius. It's about working hard and keeping at it. It's about practice and not giving up, even when your brain feels like shutting down. It's about not listening to excuses not to write.

It's also about seeing the world just a little bit differently. It's noticing that your little brother thinks 100 miles is really, really far away the same day you learned that Earth is 93 million miles from the Sun. Or that your teacher says, "Rock 'n' roll!" about 343 times a day. Maybe it's finally finding the perfect words to describe the feeling you get when you smell the hallways of your school on the first day back from summer vacation. Writing is about taking risks. You take a risk when you create a poem that expresses a feeling you're not sure you want anyone else to know about. Or a personal narrative that retells an embarrassing moment in your life. Or a story that helps you deal with a loss.

Writing is real and not just another subject to learn in school. Write. Write often. Write now. And when you're not writing, read anything you can get your hands on. **Enjoy.**

Idea Bank

Here's where you can keep all those great ideas you come up with but don't have time to write about right away.

Idea Bank

Idea Bank

Idea Bank

Words That Matter

Here are a bunch of words (and their definitions) you'll find throughout this book. Using them correctly will make you feel even more like a real writer.

Anecdote. A short, entertaining story.

Autobiography. A biography of a person written by that person.

Biography. The story of a person's life.

Blank Page Syndrome. When you want to write but can't seem to think of anything to write about.

Brainstorming. A way of finding ideas to write about.

Cliché. An expression that's used so much that you get sick and tired of it.

Conflict. Opposition between characters or other forces.

Dialogue. A conversation.

Edit. Reworking your writing for clarity and sense.

First draft. The first working version of a piece of writing.

First Draftitis. When a writer thinks her first draft is perfect just the way it is.

Flashback. When an earlier event is recounted in a story.

Freewriting. Writing down whatever comes into your head—even if you think it's dumb.

Hyperbole. Exaggerating something on purpose.

Interior monologue. When a character talks to himself (usually in his head).

J.K. Rowling. Author of the Harry Potter series.

Main character. The hero of a story.

Manuscript. A typewritten or hand-written piece of writing.

Metaphor. An imaginative comparison between two dissimilar things.

Muse. A source of inspiration.

Narrator. The voice that tells a story.

Personification. Giving human characteristics to nonhuman things.

Plot. The pattern of events in a story.

Procrastination. What writers do instead of writing.

Protagonist. The main character.

Red herring. Fake clues to distract readers.

Revise. What writers do a lot of after their first draft.

Sensory details. Descriptions that rely on any of the five senses.

Simile. A comparison between dissimilar things using like or as.

Tragic flaw. The one bad thing in an otherwise perfect hero.

Writer's block. A temporary inability to write.

Index